ORTHODOX ICON COLORING BOOK

— VOL. 2 —

17 ICONS OF JESUS AND THE SAINTS

SIMON OSKOLNIY

Printed in the United States of America
ISBN: 978-1619495395

CONTENTS

This page intentionally left blank.

3

Plate 1.
Apostle Paul by Andrei Rublev, 1410s

Plate 2.
Dormition by Anonymous, end of 15th century

Plate 3.
Saviour in Glory by Anonymous, 1408

Plate 4.
St. Tatiana by Unknown

13

Plate 6.
St. Michael by Andrei Rublev, 1408

Plate 7.
St. Gregory the Theologian by Andrei Rublev, 1408

Plate 8.
Saints Boris and Gleb by Anonymous, 15th Century

Plate 9.
St. John the Theologian by Andrei Rublev, 1408

Plate 10.
St. Nicholas with Selected Saints by Anonymous, End of 12th century

Plate 11.
St. John the Baptist by Andrei Rublev, 1408

Plate 12.
Harrowing of Hell by Andrei Rublev, 1409-1410

Plate 13.
The Crucifixion by Anonymous, 1500

Plate 14.
Miracle of Florus and Laurus by Anonymous, 15th Century

Plate 15.
Baptism by Anonymous, 1430-1440

Plate 16.
Transfiguration by Anonymous, 1400